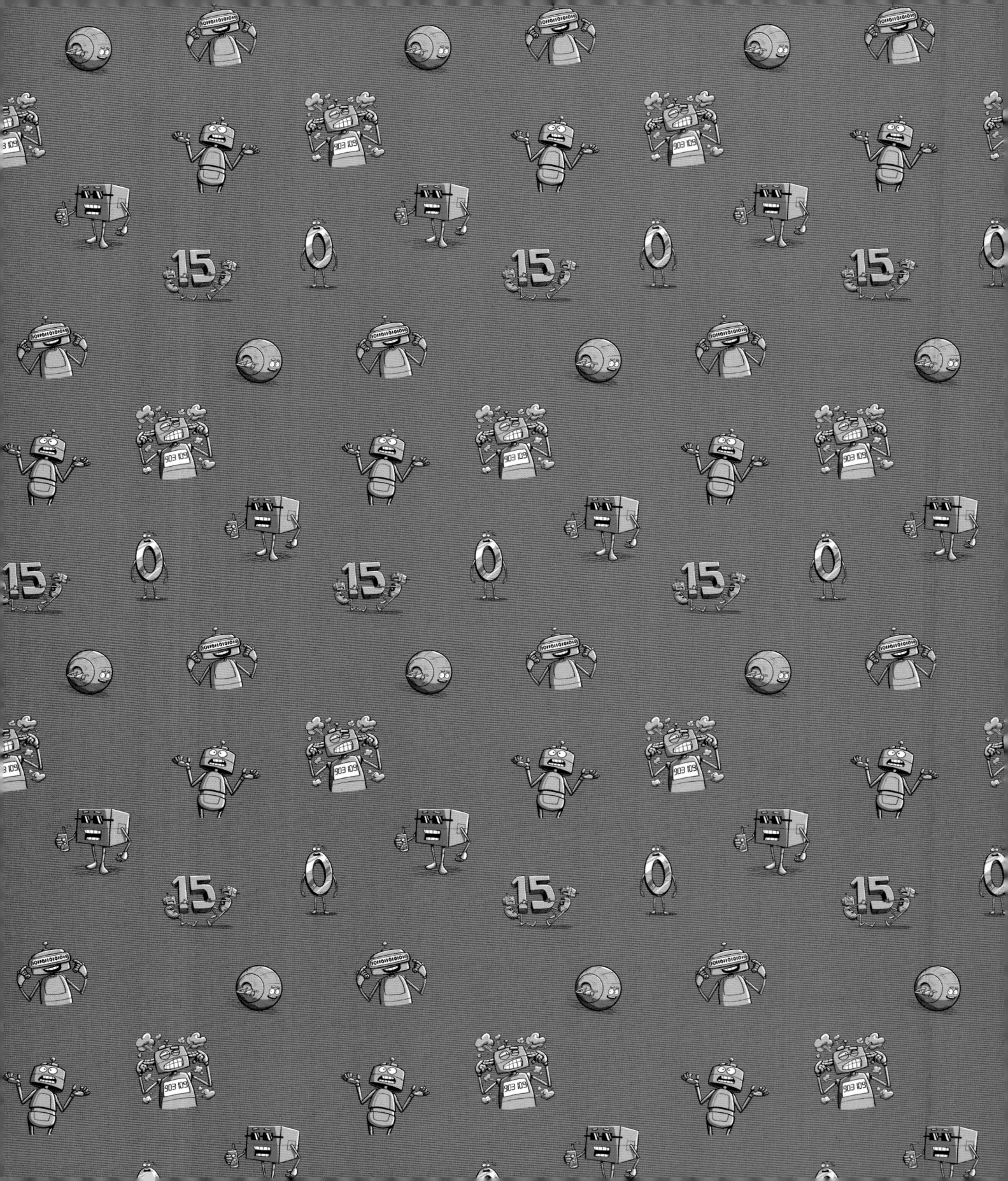

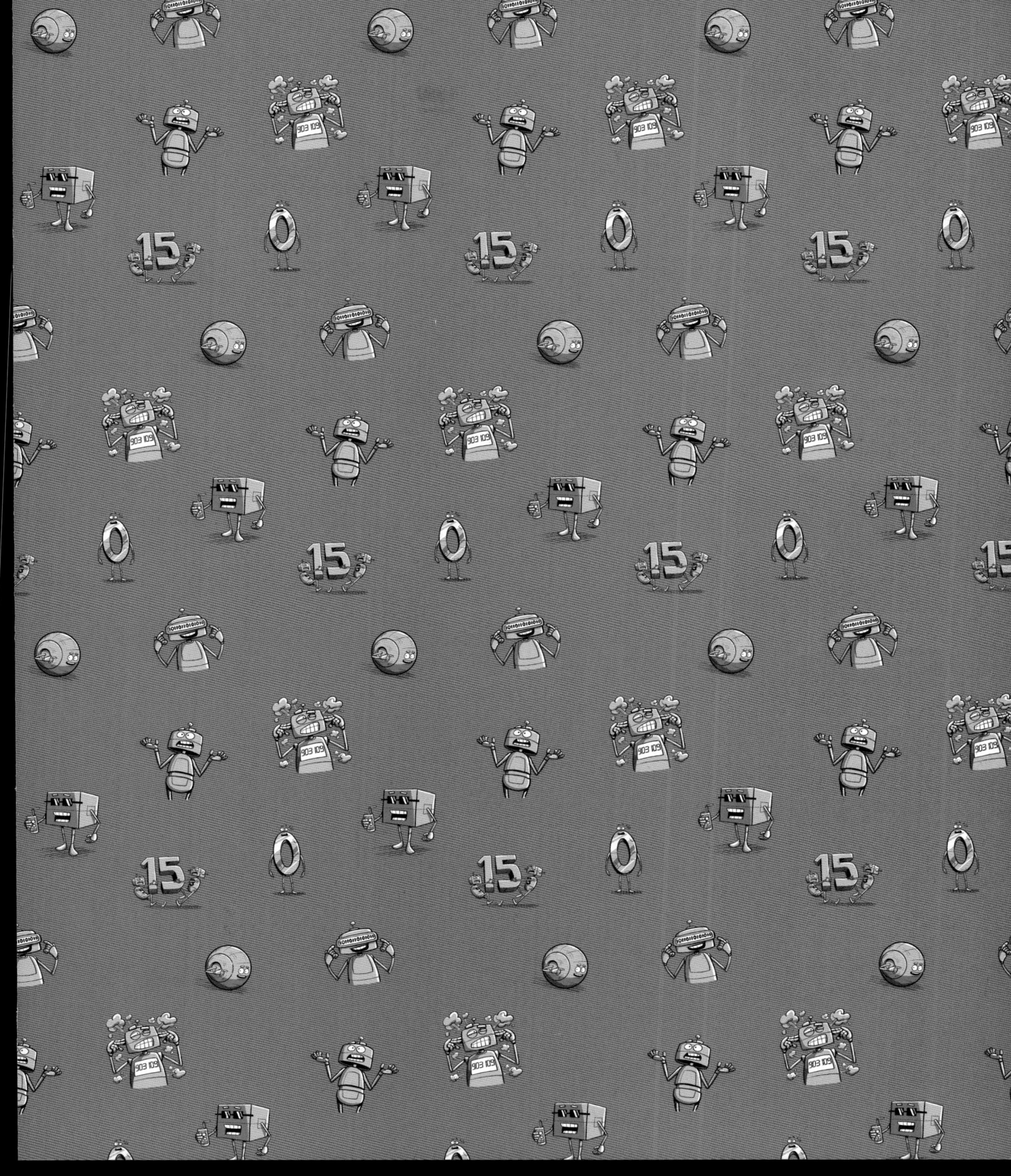

MATHS...

Is Weird!

CONTENTS

LITTLE TIGER
LONDON

CATERPILLAR BOOKS
An imprint of the Little Tiger Group
www.littletiger.co.uk
1 Coda Studios, 189 Munster Road, London SW6 6AW
Imported into the EEA by Penguin Random House Ireland,
Morrison Chambers, 32 Nassau Street, Dublin DO2 YH68
First published in Great Britain 2022
Copyright © NOODLE FUEL Ltd 2022
Text by Noodle Fuel 2022
Illustrations by Luke Newell 2022
All rights reserved • Printed in China
A CIP catalogue record of this book is available
from the British Library
ISBN: 978-1-83891-409-7
CPB/2800/2112/0122
1 3 5 7 9 10 8 6 4 2

FSC
www.fsc.org
MIX
Paper from
responsible sources
FSC® C017606

The Forest Stewardship Council® (FSC®) is an
international, non-governmental organisation
dedicated to promoting responsible management
of the world's forests. FSC operates a system of
forest certification and product labelling that
allows consumers to identify wood and wood-
based products from well-managed forests and
other controlled sources.

For more information about the FSC,
please visit their website at
www.fsc.org.

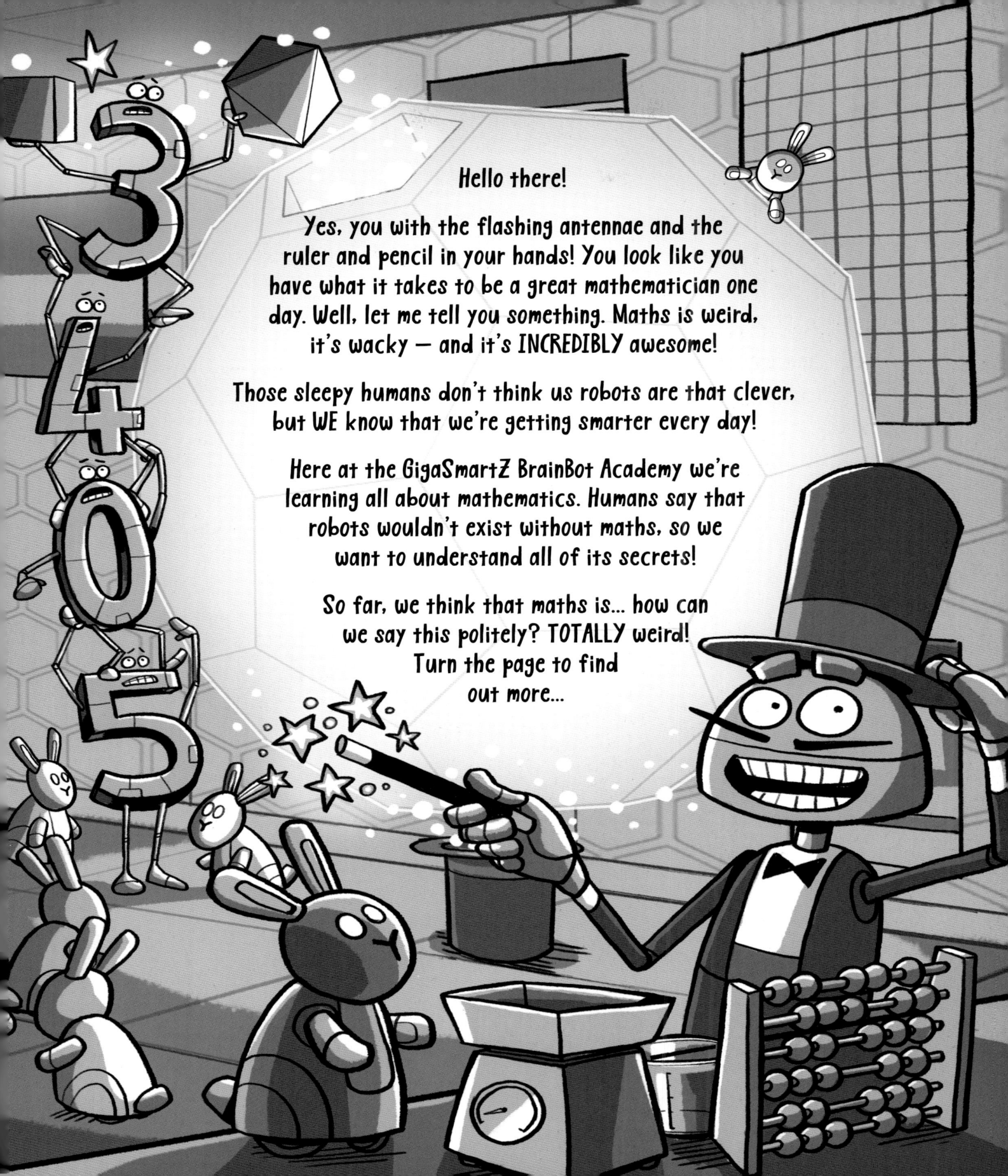

Hello there!

Yes, you with the flashing antennae and the ruler and pencil in your hands! You look like you have what it takes to be a great mathematician one day. Well, let me tell you something. Maths is weird, it's wacky — and it's INCREDIBLY awesome!

Those sleepy humans don't think us robots are that clever, but WE know that we're getting smarter every day!

Here at the GigaSmartZ BrainBot Academy we're learning all about mathematics. Humans say that robots wouldn't exist without maths, so we want to understand all of its secrets!

So far, we think that maths is... how can we say this politely? TOTALLY weird! Turn the page to find out more...

WHAT ARE NUMBERS?

Imagine a world without numbers! Numbers help you to describe quantities and measurements — such as how many stars there are in the sky or how far away the Moon is.

Thousands of years ago, early humans used their **ten fingers** to count with. Many experts believe that's why humans tend to group numbers in tens.

IT MAY ALSO EXPLAIN WHY SOME HUMANS STRUGGLE WITH ANY NUMBER BIGGER THAN TEN.

A numeral is a **symbol** that represents a number. These days, Hindu-Arabic numerals are widely used across the world. They originated in India about 1500 years ago.

Digits are the **single numerals** that go up to 9. They can be put together to make larger numbers.

A digit's position in a numeral indicates its **value**, or how much it is worth.

thousands   hundreds   tens   ones

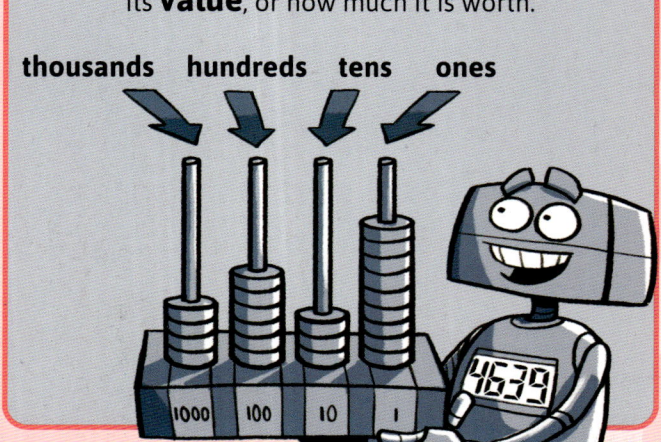

Take the number 4639.

The 9 is in the 'ones' position, so it has a value of nine ones.

The 3 is in the 'tens' place, so it is worth three tens or thirty.

The 6 is in the 'hundreds' place, so it's worth six hundreds, and the 4 is in the 'thousands' position, so it has a value of – you guessed it – four thousands.

Four thousand six hundred and thirty-nine.

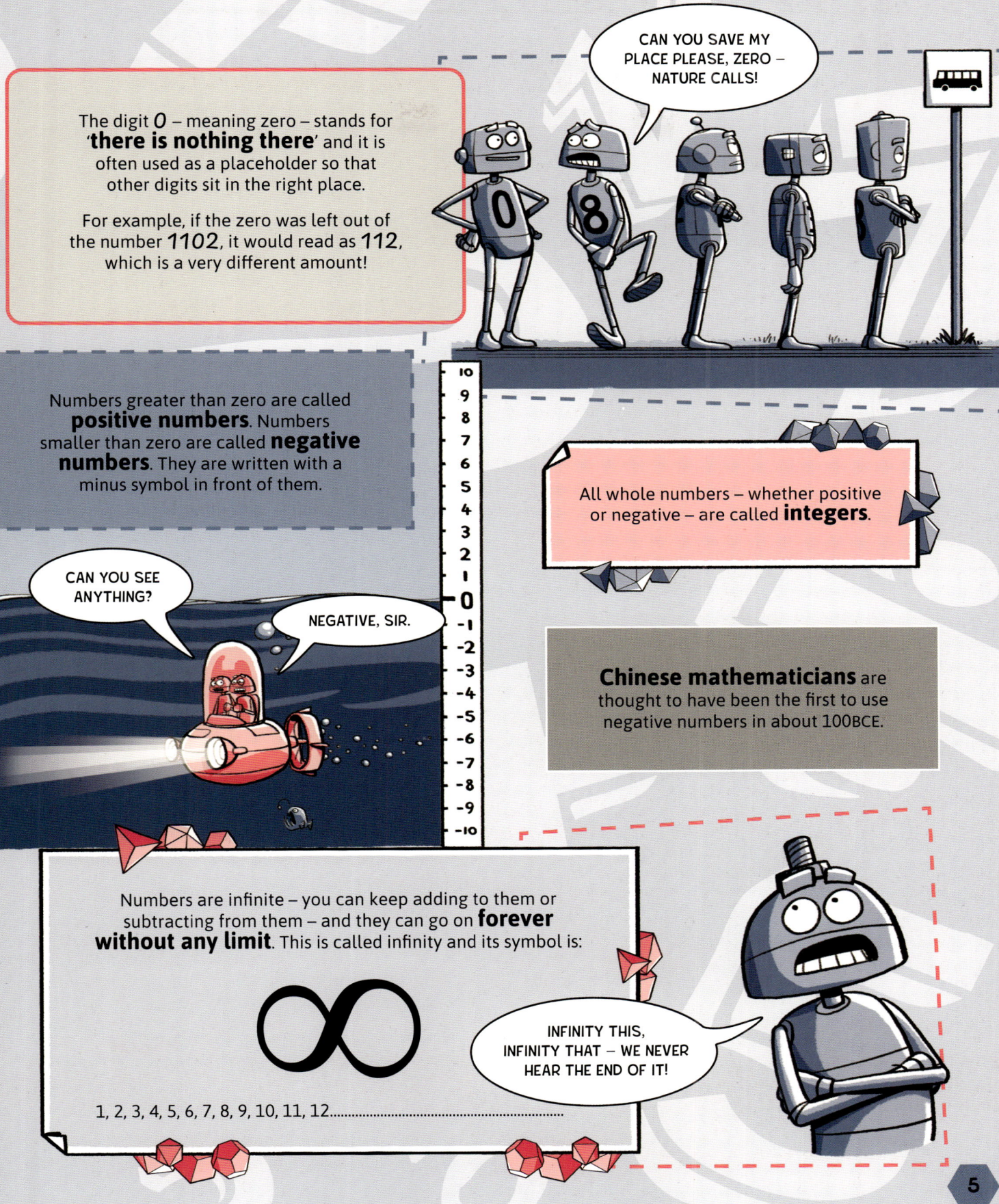

The digit *0* – meaning zero – stands for **'there is nothing there'** and it is often used as a placeholder so that other digits sit in the right place.

For example, if the zero was left out of the number 1102, it would read as 112, which is a very different amount!

CAN YOU SAVE MY PLACE PLEASE, ZERO – NATURE CALLS!

Numbers greater than zero are called **positive numbers**. Numbers smaller than zero are called **negative numbers**. They are written with a minus symbol in front of them.

All whole numbers – whether positive or negative – are called **integers**.

CAN YOU SEE ANYTHING?

NEGATIVE, SIR.

Chinese mathematicians are thought to have been the first to use negative numbers in about 100BCE.

Numbers are infinite – you can keep adding to them or subtracting from them – and they can go on **forever without any limit**. This is called infinity and its symbol is:

$$\infty$$

INFINITY THIS, INFINITY THAT – WE NEVER HEAR THE END OF IT!

1, 2, 3, 4, 5, 6, 7, 8, 9, 10, 11, 12...

ADDITION AND SUBTRACTION

Addition is about finding the total of two or more numbers. **Subtraction** is about working out what you have left when you take one number away from another.

The plus symbol '**+**' tells you to add. The minus symbol '**−**' tells you to subtract.

THEY CAN NEVER TAKE ME FROM YOU!

WE'LL SEE ABOUT THAT...

Over 2000 years ago in ancient Egypt, the symbol below meant '**plus**' if it was '**walking**' in the same direction as the hieroglyphs around it, or '**subtract**' if it was going in the opposite direction.

SUBTRACT!

Before the 16th century, the letter '*p*' stood for plus and '*m*' for minus in Europe.

Learning to add up numbers in your head is a handy skill. There are a few tricks that can help you become a **mental addition whizz**.

One tip is to split one or two of the numbers into smaller numbers first.

$$64 + 18 =$$

$$64 + 10 + 8 =$$

$$74 + 8 =$$

$$82$$

YOU'RE BREAKING UP, NUMBERS! I'M GOING TO HAVE TO CALL YOU BACK.

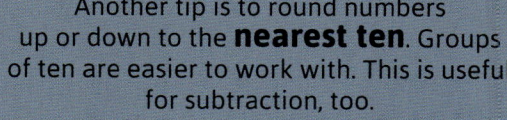

Another tip is to round numbers up or down to the **nearest ten**. Groups of ten are easier to work with. This is useful for subtraction, too.

Let's take **78 − 34**

Round up 78 to 80:

$$80 - 34 = 46$$

Then subtract the rounding up number '2':

$$46 - 2 = 44$$

So, $78 - 34 = 44$

Even simple addition can be intriguing. Can you spot the pattern in this sequence of numbers?

0, 1, 1, 2, 3, 5, 8, 13, 21, 34...?

You guessed it! Each number is the total of the two previous numbers added together. It is called the **Fibonacci sequence**, and it was first investigated by the 13th century Italian mathematician Leonardo of Pisa, also known as Fibonacci.

The fascinating Fibonacci sequence **appears in nature**, such as in the arrangement of leaves on a stem, petals on a flower and proportions of a shell.

5, 8, 13...
5, 8, 13...
5, 8, 13...

THE HARDEST PART OF LEARNING THE FIBONACCI SEQUENCE IS THE TIMING!

The number 6174, also known as **Kaprekar's constant** (after the 20th-century mathematician D R Kaprekar), is a rather sneaky number.

Write down any **four-digit number** (that contains at least two different digits). Then arrange the four digits in descending order (going down) and then again in ascending order (going up). Subtract the smaller number from the larger one. Repeat all the steps again.

Take the number 4278...

8742 - 2478 = 6264
6642 - 2466 = 4176
7641 - 1467 = 6174

Take the number 5031...

5310 - 0135 = 5175
7551 - 1557 = 5994
9954 - 4599 = 5355
5553 - 3555 = 1998
9981 - 1899 = 8082
8820 - 0288 = 8532
8532 - 2358 = 6174

You always get the number 6174 within **seven sums** and if you keep going it comes to 6174 again – and again. Weird!

Do 1, 2, 3, 4, 5, 6, 7, 8 and 9 make 100? No? Well, they do if you arrange them like this:

12 + 3 - 4 + 5 + 67 + 8 + 9 = 100

Or like this...

1 + 23 - 4 + 5 + 6 + 78 - 9 = 100

There are other ways to arrange these numbers with plus and minus signs to make a total of 100. Can you find them?

I'VE SEEN A FEW HUNDREDS IN MY TIME TOO!

SO, 6174, WE MEET AGAIN...

MULTIPLICATION

Multiplication is a calculation that is often described as repeated addition. When you multiply a number or quantity you are adding it to itself several times over.

THEY JUST KEEP MULTIPLYING!

If you have three boxes and they each contain **four custard tarts**, instead of writing:

$$4 + 4 + 4 = 12$$

to find out the total number of custard tarts, you can write:

$$3 \times 4 = 12$$

WELL, I SUPPOSE THAT WAS INEVITABLE...

The **multiplication symbol** 'x' tells you to multiply. You don't have to multiply numbers in a particular order.

$4 \times 3 = 12$ works just as well as $3 \times 4 = 12$

When you multiply numbers together you build **multiples**. Here are some multiples of four:

4 (4 x 1)   8 (4 x 2)
12 (4 x 3)   16 (4 x 4)

The **parallel lines symbol** '=' that means equals was first introduced by the Welsh mathematician Robert Recorde (c.1510–1558) 'to avoid the tedious repetition' of the words 'is equal to'.

Common multiples are multiples that are shared by more than one number. For example, 15 is a common multiple of both five and three.

SOME ARE MORE EQUAL THAN OTHERS!

IT'S MY MULTIPLE!

NO! IT'S MY MULTIPLE!

Multiplication (or times) tables help you to work out the sum of two numbers multiplied together. Once you have mastered them, you'll be the champion of all sorts of clever calculations!

The **ancient Babylonians** were probably the first people to use multiplication tables more than 4000 years ago.

You can use a **multiplication table** to work out a sum such as: **8 x 9**. First, find the column labelled 8 and the row labelled 9. The answer lies where the two lines meet: 72.

Multiplication Table

columns

X	1	2	3	4	5	6	7	8	9	10
1	1	2	3	4	5	6	7	8	9	10
2	2	4	6	8	10	12	14	16	18	20
3	3	6	9	12	15	18	21	24	27	30
4	4	8	12	16	20	24	28	32	36	40
5	5	10	15	20	25	30	35	40	45	50
6	6	12	18	24	30	36	42	48	54	60
7	7	14	21	28	35	42	49	56	63	70
8	8	16	24	32	40	48	56	64	72	80
9	9	18	27	36	45	54	63	72	81	90
10	10	20	30	40	50	60	70	80	90	100

rows

It can be incredibly useful to **multiply in your head**, and it's easier than you think.

When you multiply numbers in the hundreds or thousands, think of them as ones first and then add all the zeros:

$$500 \times 900 = ?$$

$$5 \times 9 = 45$$

So, **5**0**0 X 9**00 **= 45**0000

Another tip is to split one or more of the numbers into smaller numbers, like this:

$$8 \times 36$$

$$= (8 \times 30) + (8 \times 6)$$

$$= 240 + 48$$

$$= 288$$

PHEW! I WAS FEELING A BIT LEFT OUT THERE UNTIL THE END.

To make multiplying by 11 easier, remember that 11 is ten plus one. So, **45 x 11** is **45 x 10 (450) + 45**, which equals **495**.

If you multiply numbers that are made up of only ones, you get palindrome numbers. Palindrome numbers remain the same if you reverse the digits.

$$11 \times 11 = 121$$

$$111111 \times 111111 = 12345654321$$

Now, **choose two numbers under ten**. Let's say two and four. Add them together to get a third number (six). Then add six and four together to get a fourth number (ten). Continue this sequence, adding the largest and second-largest numbers together until you have ten numbers.

2 4 6 10 16 26 42 68 110 178 (sequence)

6   10   16   26   42   68   110   178

To quickly find the total of all ten numbers in your sequence, multiply the seventh number by 11.

In this case, **42 x 11 = 462**, and **462** is also the sum of all the numbers added together. It works every time!

THAT'S WEIRD WHICHEVER WAY YOU LOOK AT IT!

AND FOR MY NEXT TRICK...

DIVISION

When humans split a number or quantity into smaller, equal groups, they are using **division**. The symbol '÷' in a calculation tells you that it's time to start dividing!

Division is one of the **four basic mathematical operations**, along with addition, subtraction and multiplication.

I'M MAGIC AT LONG DIVISION!

THE OPERATIONS

If you have **15** new bleeping light sensors and you want to share them out equally between three of your robot pals, you divide **15** by three:

15 ÷ 3 = 5 sensors each.

Division is the **opposite** of multiplication.

So, **5 x 3 = 15** and **15 ÷ 3 = 5**

Once you know your **multiplication tables** you can work out many division sums in your head.

Let's take **63 ÷ 9**

You know that **7 x 9 = 63**, so **63 ÷ 9** must equal 7.

CHEER UP, IT MIGHT NEVER HAPPEN!

If you divide or multiply two positive numbers or two negative numbers, you always get a **positive number**.

But if one number is negative and the other is positive, the answer is always **negative**.

You can't always divide a number into **whole equal amounts**.

20 ÷ 9 = 2 with two remaining.

You call these extra numbers '**remainders**'.

So, **20 ÷ 9 = 2 remainder 2**

You can tell if a number is **divisible** (can be divided without leaving any remainder) **by two** if the number's end digit is 0, 2, 4, 6 or 8.

For example, **346 ÷ 2 = 173** and **654 ÷ 2 = 327**

Numbers that can be divided by two are called **even numbers**. Numbers that can't be divided by two are called **odd numbers**.

JUST A REMINDER TO REMEMBER THE REMAINDER!

I DON'T THINK WE SHOULD INCLUDE THREE. HE'S A BIT ODD...

A number is **divisible by ten** if its last digit is '*0*'.

750 ÷ 10 = 75

If you divide numbers that end with **0** by ten, you drop a zero:

300 ÷ 10 = 30

If you divide by a hundred, you drop two zeros:

300 ÷ 100 = 3

The number three appears to have **magical powers** when it comes to division.

If the digits in any number add up to three, or are a multiple of three, the whole number is divisible by three.

Take **2856**:

2 + 8 + 5 + 6 = 21

which is a multiple of three.

2856 ÷ 3 = 952

To **divide a number by five**, divide it by ten first, and then double the answer.

So, **230 ÷ 10 = 23**

23 x 2 = 46

230 ÷ 5 = 46

OOPS, CLUMSY!

OH, IT'S NOTHING TO WORRY ABOUT...

THREE IS THE MAGIC NUMBER!

11

WEIRD AND WONDERFUL NUMBERS

If you take a closer look at numbers, you'll find all sorts of fascinating patterns and connections between them. Mathematicians' minds really start to boggle!

Numbers that are **even** can be divided exactly by two. **Odd** numbers can't be divided wholly by two. The last digits of odd numbers are always **1, 3, 5, 7** or **9**.

EVEN IS EQUAL!

THREE'S COMPANY!

FANTASTIC FOUR!

SEVEN IS HEAVEN!

A **square number** is a number multiplied by itself. For example: **3 x 3 = 9**.

These are square numbers up to 100:

1, 4, 9, 16, 25, 36, 49, 64, 81, 100.

When you arrange square numbers as a series of dots, they form squares!

IT'S COOL TO BE SQUARE!

The ancient Greek mathematician **Archimedes** (c.287–212BCE) invented a way to express very large numbers using **powers** in order to calculate the number of grains of sand that would fill the universe!

THIS IS THE LAST TIME I COME TO THE BEACH WITH ARCHIMEDES!

37, 38, 39...

The symbol for a **number squared** is '2'.

So, **3² = 3 x 3 = 9**

This weeny digit symbol is called a power. You can use it for other numbers, not just square numbers. For example,

6 x 6 x 6 x 6 x 6

can be shortened to 6^5, which means **six to the power of five**.

Triangle numbers can be arranged as triangles formed of dots. If you add another row of dots you get the next number in the sequence.

1   3   6   10

15   21

ARE THESE TRIANGLE NUMBERS TRYING TO MAKE A POINT OR WHAT?

A **factor** is a number that divides exactly into another number. So, the factors of four are one, two and four, and the factors of eight are one, two, four and eight.

You can find out if a **two-digit number** is prime if you try to divide it by two, three, five or seven.

If you discover that it's divisible by any of these numbers, then it's not prime.

A **prime number** has just two factors – one and itself.

For example, 29 is a prime number because it can only be divided by one and 29.

One is not a prime number because it only has one factor – itself. Two is the only even prime number – all the others are odd.

THE ADVENTURES OF

OPTIMIST PRIME

HE'S ALWAYS IN SEVENTH HEAVEN!

Prime factors are numbers that are both factors and prime numbers.

The factors of 12 are one, two, three, four, six and twelve.

The prime factors of 12 are two and three.

Mathematicians think there are an **infinite amount of prime numbers**, but that they become less common as numbers get larger. Maths whizzes love the challenge of trying to discover new ones.

The prime number 619737131179 is endlessly curious. If you take any digit in the number and pair it with a digit next to it, the two-digit number you get is always prime. Strange but true!

619737131179

73   31   79

FRACTIONS

When you divide a pizza up for you and your friends to share, you are dealing with **fractions**. Fractions show how a whole thing can be cut up into equal pieces and how big or small the pieces are.

SHARE PIZZA? WHY WOULD YOU DO THAT?

The word fraction comes from the Latin *frangere*, which means '**to break**'.

Here are some common fractions:

$\frac{1}{4}$ quarter $\frac{1}{3}$ third

$\frac{1}{2}$ half $\frac{3}{4}$ three-quarters

Let's say you have a chocolate bar that has **six segments** and you want to eat one segment.

One segment is one sixth, or $\frac{1}{6}$, of the whole bar.

$\frac{1}{4}$ $\frac{1}{3}$

Simple, or vulgar, fractions are written with one number on top of another.

The bottom number is called the **denominator** and it tells you how many equal parts there are in total.

OH, SO THIS IS MY DENOMINATOR!

The top number is called the **numerator** and is the number of parts you are dealing with.

The **Eye of Horus** was an ancient Egyptian symbol for protection. Its parts were also used to represent fractions, such as $\frac{1}{2}$, $\frac{1}{4}$, $\frac{1}{8}$ and $\frac{1}{16}$ of *hekats*, which were units for measuring grain.

WHOA! THAT QUARTER IS REALLY EYEBALLING ME!

A mixed number is a whole number and a fraction together, such as $3\frac{6}{8}$.

A **proper fraction** has a numerator that is smaller than a denominator: $\frac{7}{15}$.

An **improper fraction** has a numerator that is bigger than a denominator: $\frac{20}{12}$.

OH, I KNOW HOW THAT FEELS.

Sometimes it's difficult to tell how big or small a fraction is at first. You can **simplify it** by finding a number that both the numerator and the denominator are divisible by.

Take $\frac{16}{24}$

16 and 24 are divisible by 4.

$$\frac{16}{24} \div \frac{4}{4} = \frac{4}{6}$$

4 and 6 are divisible by 2.

$$\frac{4}{6} \div \frac{2}{2} = \frac{2}{3}$$

So, $\frac{16}{24}$ can be simplified to $\frac{2}{3}$.

DID ANYONE ACTUALLY ASK $\frac{16}{24}$ IF IT WANTED TO BE SIMPLIFIED?

If you want to compare two different fractions, first of all, multiply the two denominators by each other.

$$\frac{3}{4} \qquad \frac{6}{9}$$

4 x 9 = 36, so make 36 the new denominator.

Multiply each numerator by the original denominator of the other fraction:

3 x 9 = 27 and **6 x 4 = 24**

$$\frac{3}{4} = \frac{27}{36}$$

$$\frac{6}{9} = \frac{24}{36}$$

Now we can see that $\frac{3}{4}$ is a **bigger** fraction than $\frac{6}{9}$.

To find **the quantity** that a fraction represents – for instance, how many robots make up $\frac{2}{5}$ of the ten members of the Digital Droners choir...

Divide 10 by the denominator:

10 ÷ 5 = 2

Multiply your answer by the numerator:

2 x 2 = 4

So $\frac{2}{5}$ of the choir = **4** singers.

DIGITAL DRONERS

ERR, I DON'T THINK SO. YOU'RE A ROBOT – YOU DON'T WORK WITH FRACTIONS; YOU USE DECIMALS...

I COULD DO THIS IN A FRACTION OF THE TIME!

DECIMALS

Decimals show numbers that lie in between whole numbers. You can spot them because they have a dot called a decimal point. The numbers *11.5*, *49.79* and *14.837* are all examples of decimals.

Decimals express the value of a unit divided into **fractions of ten** – or **tenths** ($\frac{1}{10}$). The tenths can be divided by ten again into hundredths of whole numbers – and then into thousandths, and so on.

27.516

| tens | ones | point | tenths | hundredths | thousandths |

You place the **decimal point** between the whole number and the smaller parts that make up that number.

The position of digits after the decimal point is called the decimal place.

0.1 = one decimal place

0.13 = two decimal places

0.137 = three decimal places

The 16th century Flemish mathematician **Simon Stevin** helped to popularise decimals in Europe. He thought they were easier to do calculations with than fractions.

DECIMALS, NOT DECIBELS!

YEAH, I'M WITH YOU, BROTHER!

Fractions can be converted into decimals by dividing the numerator by the denominator.

Sometimes you get decimals that are **recurring** – the digits after the decimal point go on forever!

0.3333... (or $\frac{1}{3}$) is a recurring decimal.

Today, not all countries use a '.' for a decimal point symbol. Many use a **comma** instead.

YOU CAN'T ALL COME IN!

16

These are common decimal and fraction equivalents:

$$0.75 = \frac{3}{4} \qquad 0.5 = \frac{1}{2}$$

$$0.25 = \frac{1}{4} \qquad 0.1 = \frac{1}{10}$$

$$0.01 = \frac{1}{100} \qquad 0.001 = \frac{1}{1000}$$

Now for a **fun calculator sum**! Enter any digit from *1* to *8*. Then divide it by *9*. You always get a decimal filled with the digit you pressed in the first place!

Not all numbers can be divided into simple fractions. Those that can't are called **irrational numbers**. As decimals, the digits of irrational numbers go on forever, without repeating. **Pi (π)** is an irrational number.

$$\pi = 3.1415926535897932384...$$

THE EARTH IS FLAT!

YOU'RE JUST BEING IRRATIONAL!

The decimal system is based on groups of ten, but computers work differently.

When they organise and store information, they use **binary code**. They count with just two digits: *0* and *1*.

0 is an **off** electrical signal, and *1* is an **on** signal.

Most countries of the world have **currencies** (money systems) that are based on decimals, with units that are divided into hundredths.

A **British pound (£)** is made up of one hundred pence and a **US dollar ($)** is made up of one hundred cents.

£5.19 (five pounds and 19 pence) =

5 and *19* hundredths.

Values that are smaller than a dollar or pound are also written as decimals: *£0.19*

or as a whole number of pence or cents: *19p*.

NOW YOU'RE TALKING MY LANGUAGE!

THERE ARE VALUES SMALLER THAN A DOLLAR?

17

PERCENTAGES

Percentages, like fractions and decimals, describe a proportion of a whole. 'Percent' means 'out of one hundred', so the whole in percentages is made up of a hundred equal parts.

The symbol '**%**' represents a percentage. It is a shortened form of the Italian words for percent – *per cento*.

If **65%** of people have an ice cream at the seaside, that's equivalent to 65 out of **100**, or $\frac{65}{100}$ or **0.65**.

5%

IT'S BEEN A LONG DAY – BETTER RECHARGE!

Over 2,000 years ago in **ancient Rome**, long before the decimal system, people were charged a $\frac{1}{100}$, or **1%** tax.

THAT WILL BE 1% PLEASE, CENT-URION!

When you want to find the quantity that **a percentage represents**, it's helpful to work out what **1%** is first.

Let's say there are **150** competitors at a sports day and **20%** take part in the hurdles race...

To figure out how many competitors there are in the hurdles race, divide **150** by **100** to find **1%**:

150 ÷ 100 = 1.5

Then, multiply 1.5 by 20 to get the number of hurdlers:

1.5 x 20 = 30

So, **20%** = 30 hurdlers.

MAYBE THE HURDLES RACE WASN'T THE RIGHT EVENT FOR TANKBOT...

To change a **decimal** into a percentage, multiply the decimal by 100.

0.73 x 100 = 73%

DON'T YOU MULTIPLY BY 100!

There are eight houses in a street and two of them have **pink doors**.

To work out what percentage of the houses have pink doors, divide the number of pink doors by the total number of doors, then multiply by 100.

Simplify the fraction first, before turning it into a decimal number.

$$\frac{2}{8} \times 100 = \frac{1}{4} \times 100$$
$$= 0.25 \times 100 = 25\%$$

When you've been to the shops during the sales, have you noticed that products have **discount labels**, such as **10%** or **25%** off?

To work out the cheaper price, find the value of the percentage discount, then take it away from the original price.

A pair of trainers is reduced by **25%** from their original price of **£50.00**.

For every **£1.00** you would normally pay, take **25p** off.

So, **50 x £0.25 = £12.50** is the amount that you take off the full price.

The sale price for the trainers, then, is **£37.50**.

Some bank accounts pay **interest** if you save money in them. Interest is an amount of money based on a percentage known as an interest rate.

If the interest rate is **2%** per year and you saved **£100**, after a year the bank would give you **£2** (**100 x 0.02**), so you would have **£102**.

THE CHEAPER THE BETTER, TO BE HONEST!

BANKS GIVING AWAY MONEY – NOW THAT IS INTERESTING!

RATIOS

Humans love to bake things like cakes, muffins and cheese straws.

When they measure baking ingredients, they are working with **ratios**. Ratios compare one part of a whole with another.

Let's say you are baking bread and the ratio of flour to water is 5:3. This means that you mix **five parts of flour to three parts of water**. Even if you are making truckloads of bread and using larger quantities, the proportion of flour to water is always the same.

THE RATIO WAS RIGHT; QUANTITIES MIGHT HAVE BEEN A BIT OFF THOUGH...

You can use ratios to describe **other types of proportions**, too.

If your robodog has had **puppies** and three puppies are silver and one puppy is black, the ratio of silver to black puppies is 3:1.

WALKIES, PUPS! TIME TO POWER UP!

Maps make use of ratios to show distances. To fit a large area on a map, you have to shrink it down on the page. Kilometres or miles are converted to much smaller units, such as centimetres or inches.

One centimetre on the page may represent a distance of **100000cm** or **1km**. This is described as a size ratio, or scale, of **1:100000**.

Suppose that you have **100** new circuit boards and you want to share them out between you and your friend, at a ratio of **2:3**.

First, work out the number of parts – that's:

2 + 3 = 5

Then divide the total number of circuit boards by five, to find the value for each part:

100 ÷ 5 = 20

So, you have **40** circuit boards (**2 x 20**), and your friend has **60** (**3 x 20**).

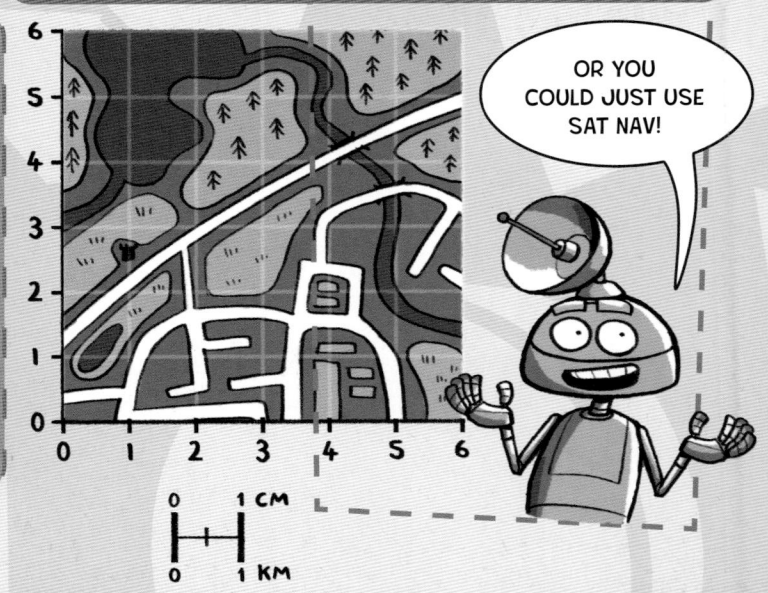

OR YOU COULD JUST USE SAT NAV!

PROBABILITY

What is the likelihood of it raining tomorrow? Or of a meteor striking Earth? Or of you meeting a human that can fly? These are all examples of probability – the chance of something happening.

If there is **no chance** of an event happening, the probability is said to be **zero or 0%**. If something is certain, the probability is **one or 100%**.

WHAT'S THE PROBABILITY OF HUMANS FINDING ALL THE PRIME NUMBERS?

ZILCH!

The Swiss mathematician Jacob Bernoulli (1655–1705) came up with the **law of large numbers**, which says that over a long time the outcomes of events are reasonably predictable. For instance, if you toss a coin, it may seem that you get more heads or more tails in the first few tosses, but after a thousand tosses, about half will have landed as heads and half as tails.

You might have heard people mention a **one in two chance** or a **50:50 chance**. They are both ways of expressing an equally likely outcome.

When you toss a coin, there are two possible outcomes – heads or tails. The probability of it landing either as heads or as tails is $\frac{1}{2}$ – or a **one in two chance**.

If you throw the coin again you have the same probability of outcome as before, but the chance of throwing two heads or two tails in a row is:

$$\frac{1}{2} \times \frac{1}{2} = \frac{1}{4}$$

(That's right, you multiply the individual probabilities.)

FIRST TOSS	SECOND TOSS	OUTCOME	PROBABILITY
	$\frac{1}{2}$ H	HH	$\frac{1}{2} \times \frac{1}{2} = \frac{1}{4}$
$\frac{1}{2}$ H	$\frac{1}{2}$		
	$\frac{1}{2}$ T	HT	$\frac{1}{2} \times \frac{1}{2} = \frac{1}{4}$
0	$\frac{1}{2}$ H	TH	$\frac{1}{2} \times \frac{1}{2} = \frac{1}{4}$
$\frac{1}{2}$ T	$\frac{1}{2}$		
T	$\frac{1}{2}$ T	TT	$\frac{1}{2} \times \frac{1}{2} = \frac{1}{4}$

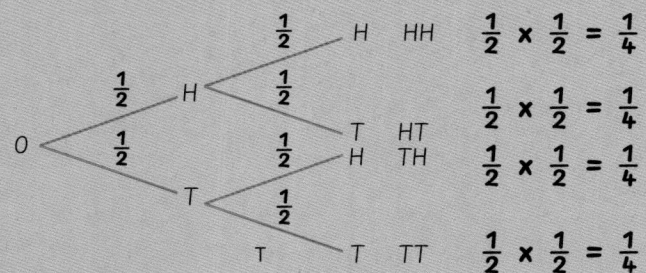

HEADS OR TAILS?

WE'RE NEVER GOING TO GET THIS MATCH STARTED AT THIS RATE.

I'M NOT SURE, TO BE HONEST!

Here's something to ponder – in a random group of **23** people there's a **50%** chance that two of the people will **share the same birthday**. In a room of **75** people, it's a **99.9%** chance. Weird!

AVERAGES

THAT'S A LOT OF PIZZAS!

An **average** is a typical value in a set of values. It might be, for example, the average daily temperature in a week or the average number of **pizza deliveries** a robot has made in a month.

A **mean average** is the total of all the values added together, divided by the number of values there are.

MY PROGRAMMER SAID I WAS VERY AVERAGE.

WELL, THAT'S A BIT MEAN!

$$5 + 25 + 60 + 5 + 15 = 110 \qquad 110 \div 5 = 22$$

So, the mean number of pizza deliveries made a month is 22.

The **mode** is the value in a list that appears the most often. So, **five pizza deliveries** is the mode average.

To find the median in an **even number of values**, place them in order, add the middle two values together and divide the result by two.

5 15 15 20 25 40

$$15 + 20 = 35$$

$$35 \div 2 = 17.5$$

So, the median is 17.5.

The **median** is the middle value in a list. To find it, you write all the values out in order from smallest to largest, and choose the value that lies in the middle.

HIDING IN THE MIDDLE? WHAT A CO-MEDIAN!

THEY ALL LOOK THE SAME TO ME!

5 5 (15) 25 60

So, the median number of pizza deliveries is 15.

Values in a list that are much smaller or bigger than all the others are called **outliers**. They can distort a mean average, making it strangely high or low.

When you have an outlier in a list, it's best to use a median average to get a more typical average figure.

Take these figures for the number of tasty megabytes that **each robot munched** through in a week:

7 12 5 3 60 9 6

60 is much bigger than all the other figures, so you should use the median average to find the typical number. Don't forget to reorder the numbers!

3 5 6 (7) 9 12 60

The median average is 7 because it is the middle number in the range.

OH, JUST IGNORE BOB. HE'S SUCH AN OUTLIER...

Here's a way to remember **each type of average**: mode sounds like 'most', median sounds like 'medium' and 'mean' is the one that's left!

The **range** of a list of values is the difference between the smallest and largest numbers.

Let's say the GigaSmartZ BrainBot Academy has a quiz night.

EVERYONE DISCONNECTED FROM THE INTERNET? GREAT! QUESTION ONE...

The team scores were as follows: 6 25 17 9 16 30.

Put them in order: 6 9 16 17 25 30.

The range is **30 – 6 = 24**.

Averages can be staggering facts! Did you know that on average, humans produce **1–1.5l** (34-51fl oz) of mucus and phlegm a day to clear their noses and throats?

GROSS! THAT WOULD RUST OUR INSIDES!

23

MEASURING

Whether you want to know the length of your pet dog's tail, the weight of your birthday cake or how long it takes you to scoot around the block, measuring is a useful skill to have!

When you describe a measurement, don't forget to include a unit of measurement. Instead of simply writing *50*, write *50m* or *50km* or whatever the unit is. Otherwise, there's confusion!

WHOA, I'M 24!

ARE YOU GOING TO TELL HIM THAT'S HIS IQ, OR AM I?

Capacity is a measure of how much something can hold. It might be the amount of soft drink in a can or the amount of dust that a hoover can contain.

Sometimes when you measure something, you get a long number that is **more accurate** than you need. If it's a decimal number, it can be easier to use if you round it to one decimal place.

Check the second digit after the decimal point. If it is **5** or over, add **1** to the digit to the left of it. If it is below **5**, leave the digit to the left as is.

So, *14.7562kg* rounded to one decimal place, for example, is *14.8kg*.

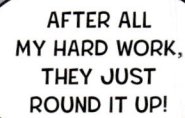

AFTER ALL MY HARD WORK, THEY JUST ROUND IT UP!

Units of Time	1 SECOND	1 MINUTE	1 HOUR	1 DAY	1 WEEK	1 YEAR
		=	=	=	=	=
		60 SECONDS	60 MINUTES	24 HOURS	7 DAYS	52 WEEKS

A year (*365 days*, or *366 days* in a leap year) is the time it takes for the Earth to orbit the Sun. A day (*24 hours*) is how long it takes the Earth to rotate once around its axis.

During the 1790s the French experimented with a metric system to measure time. It had **10 hours in a day**, **100 minutes in an hour** and **100 seconds in a minute**. But it didn't go down too well, and it was dropped after about a year.

IF ONLY THEY'D USED THE BINARY SYSTEM!

The way that humans measure hours within a day stems back to the **ancient Egyptians**. They divided day and night into 12 hours each.

In ancient times, people used to use **body parts** to measure length. A cubit was the distance along the arm from the elbow to the end of the middle finger. A span was the width of a hand and a digit was the width of a finger.

Today, most countries use the **metric measuring system**, which is based on tens, hundredths and thousandths.

The **imperial system of measurements** is older and has units such as inches (in), feet (ft), ounces (oz) and pounds (lb).

The French introduced the **metric system** to Europe during the French Revolution in the 1790s. They decided that the length of a metre should be one ten-millionth of the shortest distance from the equator to the North Pole passing through Paris.

METRIC SYSTEM

Units of Length

1 MILLIMETRE	1 CENTIMETRE	1 METRE	1 KILOMETRE
(MM)	(CM)	(M)	(KM)
	1CM = 10MM	1M = 100CM	1KM = 1000M

Units of Weight

1 MILLIGRAM	1 GRAM	1 KILOGRAM	1 TONNE
(MG)	(G)	(KG)	(T)
	1G = 1000MG	1KG = 1000G	1T = 1000KG

Units of Capacity

1 MILLILITRE	1 CENTILITRE	1 LITRE
(ML)	(CL)	(L)
	1CL = 100ML	1L = 1000ML

IMPERIAL SYSTEM

Units of Length

1 INCH	1 FOOT	1 YARD	1 MILE
(IN)	(FT)	(YD)	(MI)
	1FT = 12IN	1YD = 3FT	1MI = 1760YD

Units of Weight

1 OUNCE	1 POUND	1 STONE	1 HUNDRED-WEIGHT	1 TON
(OZ)	(LB)	(ST)	(CWT)	(TON)
	1LB = 16OZ	1ST = 14LB	1CWT = 8ST	1 TON = 20CWT

Units of Capacity

1 FLUID OUNCE	1 PINT	1 GALLON
(FL OZ)	(PT)	(GAL)
	1PT = 20FL OZ	1GAL = 8PT

I'M SORRY BUT THIS IS WHERE I DRAW THE LINE.

DON'T BE THAT WEIGH ABOUT IT.

OH, KEEP THE VOLUME DOWN, YOU TWO!

You can measure all sorts of different things, from temperature, energy and power, to the **spiciness of a chilli** or the amount of memory a computer has.

CIRCLES

Look around and you'll see circles everywhere. Wheels, doughnuts, the pupils of eyes, the Sun... It's no surprise that humans love these curious, cornerless shapes!

A circle is a closed curve with equal distance from its centre to every point on its edge. Ancient Greek and medieval scholars thought that the circle was so perfect that it might have **divine powers**!

An **arc** is a section of the circumference.

The **circumference** is the total distance around the edge of a circle.

The **radius** is the distance from the edge of a circle to its centre.

A **chord** is a straight line that has two end points on a circle.

The **diameter** of a circle is the distance from one side of it to the other through the middle. The diameter is therefore twice the length of the radius.

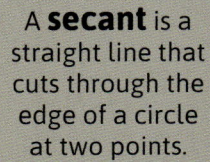

WELL I'VE MADE A GREAT SECANT, BUT I STILL CAN'T GET THE ORANGE JUICE OUT!

WILL YOU STOP THAT!

A **secant** is a straight line that cuts through the edge of a circle at two points.

A **tangent** is a line that touches a circle at one point.

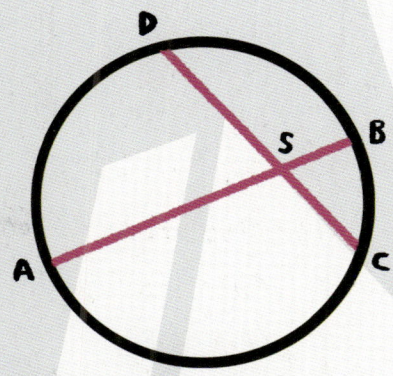

The ancient Greek philosopher **Thales of Miletus** (c.624–548BCE) noticed something interesting about chords...

1. Mark a dot anywhere inside a circle and call it S.

2. Then draw a straight line across the circle through S to form a chord. Call the chord $A-B$.

3. Measure the lines $A-S$ and $S-B$ and multiply the numbers together. Then draw another chord passing through S and call it $C-D$.

4. Measure $C-S$ and $S-D$ and multiply them together.

5. If you measure carefully, you'll find that $C-S \times S-D$ is the same as $A-S \times S-B$!

Pi is an **irrational number**, which means it's infinite and its digits don't repeat. To make calculations easier, it is often shortened to 3.14. As a fraction it is sometimes expressed as $\frac{22}{7}$.

JUST CHECKING IT TASTES THE SAME ALL THE WAY AROUND!

Pi is an intriguing number that you always get when you divide the circumference of a circle by its diameter.

$$3.14159...$$

This number is always the same, no matter how big the circle is. Its symbol is π – the Greek letter 'pi'.

$$circumference \div diameter = \pi$$
$$= 3.14159$$

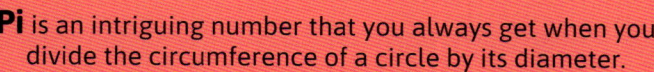

circumference

diameter

radius

To find a circle's approximate circumference, you can multiply its diameter by 3.14. So, if a circle's diameter is $20cm$, its circumference would be:

$$3.14 \times 20 = 62.8cm.$$

OH, I KNOW HOW HE FELT! SOMETIMES I JUST CAN'T STOP CALCULATING!

Strangely, if you enter 3.14 into a calculator and look at it in the mirror, it says **PIE**. Weird!

The Greek mathematician **Archimedes** loved working with shapes, and he worked hard to prove the theory of pi. It's said that he was killed by a Roman soldier because he refused to be distracted from drawing mathematical shapes in the sand.

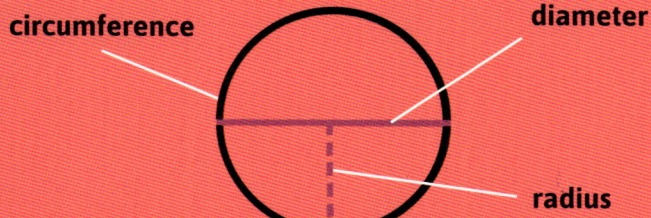

PERIMETER, AREA AND VOLUME

How do you measure the size of a sports field, a TV or a new spaceship? It all falls into place when you learn how to work out perimeters, areas and volumes.

A **perimeter** is the distance around the edge of a shape – the length of each of its sides added together.

6cm

4cm   4cm

6cm

Perimeter = 4cm + 6cm + 4cm + 6cm = 20cm

The perimeter of the **Pentagon building** in Washington, USA, is 1405m (4609ft). Each of its five sides measures 281m (921ft).

An **object's area** is the size of its surface. Area is measured in square units, such as square centimetres – also called 'centimetre squared' (**cm²**).

If you want to find the area of a rectangle or square, you **multiply its length by its width**.

The area of Russia is a huge 17098242km² (6601668sq mi). No wonder it's the **biggest country** on Earth!

The area of **world-class football fields**, such as the pitch at Wembley Stadium in the UK, is 7140m² (76854sq ft).

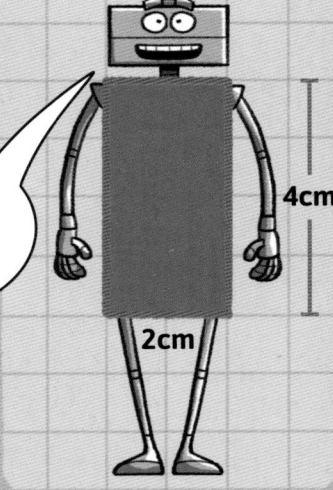

DOES MY CHASSIS LOOK BIG IN THIS?

4cm

2cm

4cm x 2cm = 8cm²

The **area of a circle** is π x radius² (π x r x r) or πr² for short. Compared to other shapes with the same perimeter, circles have the biggest area.

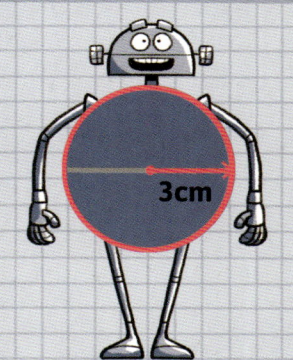

3cm

$3.14 \times 3cm \times 3cm = 28.26cm^2$

The circular base of the **Colosseum** in Rome, Italy, where gladiatorial battles once took place, is 24000m² (258000sq ft).

LOOKS LIKE SOMEONE'S TAKEN A SLICE OUT OF THAT PIE!

Volume is the amount of space that an object takes up. It is measured in cubic units, such as cubic centimetres – **cm³** – also called 'centimetre cubed'.

To find the volume of a box shape, known as a cuboid, **multiply its length by its width and its depth**.

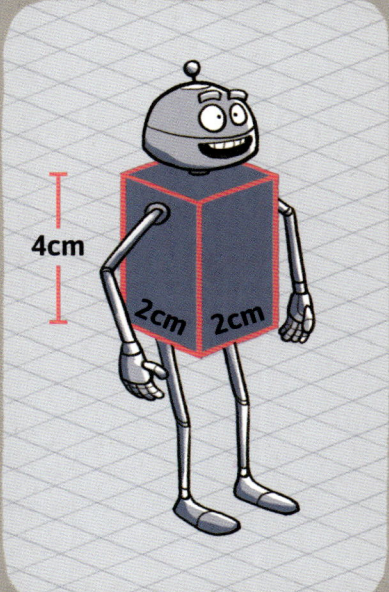

4cm
2cm **2cm**

$4cm \times 2cm \times 2cm = 16cm^3$

The volume of the **Great Pyramid of Giza** in Egypt is about 2300000m³ (81200000cu ft).

That's a lot of stone blocks (and space for mummies!).

CARRYING BLOCKS IS EASY IF YOU WALK LIKE A HIEROGLYPH!

ANGLES

From corners and hinges to the slant of your antennae, angles are everywhere. An angle is a measure of the turn between two lines that meet. It is measured in degrees, which have the symbol '°'.

A complete turn – a **full circle** – measures 360°. You can see this on a protractor, an instrument used for measuring angles. A half-turn is 180°.

A **right angle** measures 90° and is a quarter of a turn.

An angle smaller than 90° is called an **acute angle**.

I DON'T THINK I'M MADE TO BEND THIS WAY!

OOOF! THIS IS HARD WORK!

An angle between 90° and 180° is **obtuse**.

An angle that is greater than 180° is **reflex**.

ALL THIS STRETCHING IS STARTING TO HURT!

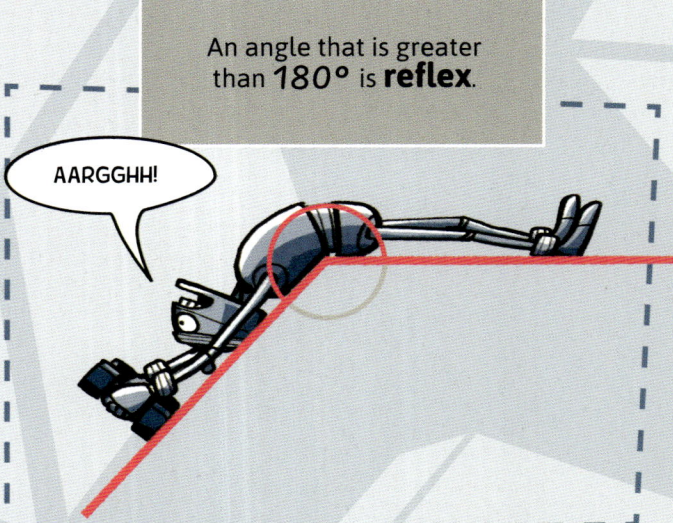

AARGGHH!

The point where two lines join is called a **vertex**.

Angles belong to a branch of maths called **geometry**. Geometry is about the measurement of space and the distance between points in shapes.

The word 'geometry' comes from the ancient Greek *gē*, meaning **earth** and *metron* meaning **measure**.

An ancient Greek mathematician named Euclid, who lived in the 4th century BCE, is sometimes called the **Father of Geometry**. He wrote *Elements*, a collection of books about maths and geometry that was still used as a textbook over 2000 years later!

The three angles inside a **triangle** always add up to *180°*.

THIS YOGA CLASS WAS SUPPOSED TO BE FOR BEGINNERS!

THEY GROW UP SO FAST!

The four angles inside a **quadrilateral** (four-sided shape) always add up to *360°*.

Geometry is used in jobs such as **engineering** and **architecture** and for navigation.

WHERE DID I PUT MY PROTRACTOR AGAIN?

WE HAVE MORE IN COMMON THAN I THOUGHT!

TRIANGLES

A triangle, with its three sides, is the simplest flat, or 2D (two-dimensional) shape. The word 'triangle' comes from the Latin *triangulus*, meaning three-cornered or angled.

Humans think that **triangles** are terrific. You see them in all sorts of places – in roofs, in road signs, in windows... and in crisps.

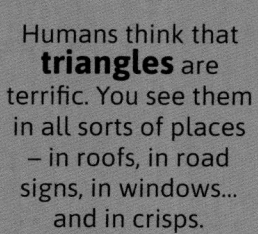

ROBOTS DON'T EAT CRISPS, BUT THEY DO LIKE SILICON CHIPS!

As part of a structure, such as a bridge, a triangle can be a **strong shape** because each of its sides supports the other two sides.

The **Eiffel Tower** in Paris, France, has a framework made up of triangles, making it super sturdy.

An **equilateral triangle** has sides that are all of equal length. Its three angles are also identical – 60°.

TRUE EQUALITY! PERFECTION!

An **isosceles triangle** has two equal sides and two equal angles. 'Isosceles' comes from the Greek *isos*, meaning **equal**, and *skelos*, meaning **leg**.

CALL THOSE LEGS?

A **right-angled triangle** has one angle that is 90° (a right angle). The longest side of a right-angled triangle is called the **hypotenuse**, and it is always opposite the right angle.

I'M HITTING THE SLOPES!

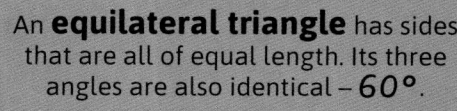
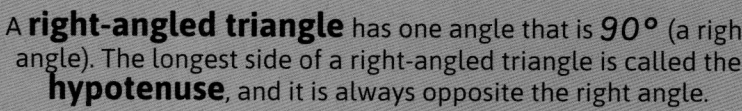

A **scalene triangle** has sides and angles that are all different.

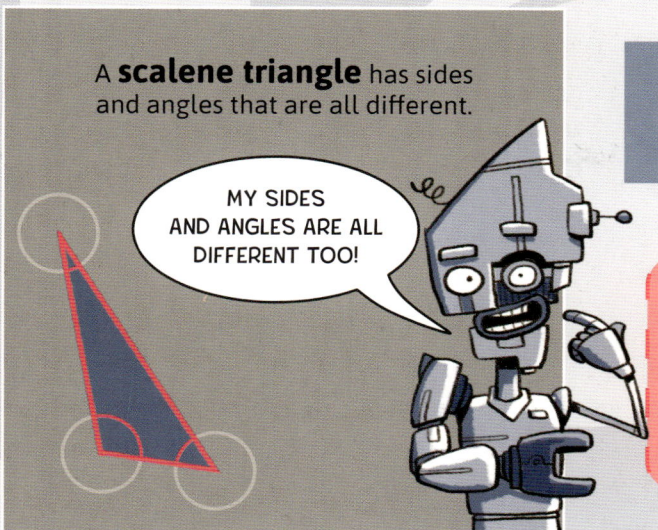

MY SIDES AND ANGLES ARE ALL DIFFERENT TOO!

The **total length of two sides** of a triangle is always longer than the third side.

The ancient Greek philosopher and mathematician **Pythagoras** (c.570–495BCE) studied triangles and he made an astonishing discovery – now known as **Pythagoras' theorem**.

Pythagoras' theorem states that in a right-angled triangle, the hypotenuse squared (multiplied by itself) is **equal to the sum of the squares of the other two sides**.

It's written as a statement like this:

$$a^2 + b^2 = c^2$$

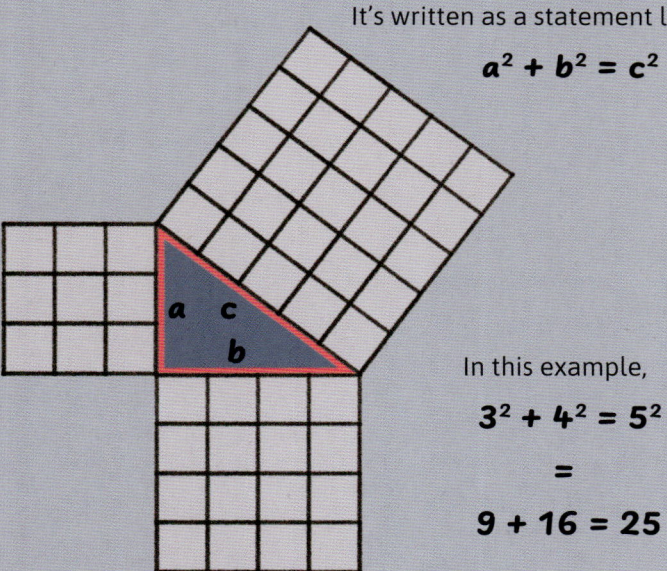

In this example,

$$3^2 + 4^2 = 5^2$$
$$=$$
$$9 + 16 = 25$$

If you know the lengths of two sides of a **right-angled triangle**, you can use Pythagoras' theorem to work out the length of the third side.

YOU CAN'T FOOL ME HUMANS – PYTHAGORAS IS OBVIOUSLY A ROBOT NAME!

Actually, it's likely that the **ancient Babylonians and Chinese** had some idea about this handy rule centuries before Pythagoras – but he proved it.

Pythagoras also founded a religion centred on maths and did not like the idea of **eating beans**!

POLYGONS

Polygons are 2D shapes with straight sides. They might not have thickness or depth, but there is definitely more to them than meets the eye.

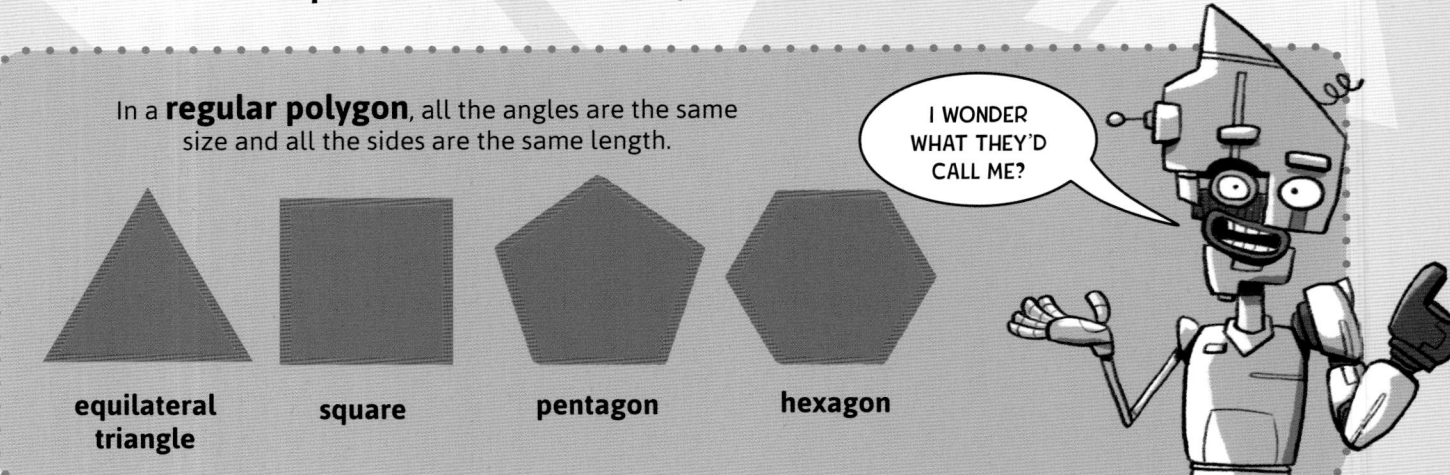

In a **regular polygon**, all the angles are the same size and all the sides are the same length.

I WONDER WHAT THEY'D CALL ME?

equilateral triangle

square

pentagon

hexagon

Irregular polygons have sides and angles of different lengths and sizes.

Polygons are named after the number of angles and sides that they have. For instance, a **six-sided shape** is called a hexagon after the ancient Greek *hex* for **six** and *gonu* for **knee** or **angle**.

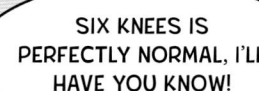

SIX KNEES IS PERFECTLY NORMAL, I'LL HAVE YOU KNOW!

The **US Department of Defence HQ** – the Pentagon – is famous for being five-sided. It's made up of five pentagonal rings, one inside another, that are connected by ten spoke-like corridors, making it easy for people to walk from one end of the large building to the other.

A regular polygon is **symmetrical**, which means that if you draw a line across it, it can divide into identical sections. It has the same number of lines of symmetry as it has sides.

YOU CAN'T IMPROVE ON PERFECTION!

All polygons can be **split into triangles**. Intriguingly, the smallest number of triangles you can find in a polygon is always two fewer than the number of the polygon's sides. So, for an eight-sided polygon (octagon), you get six triangles.

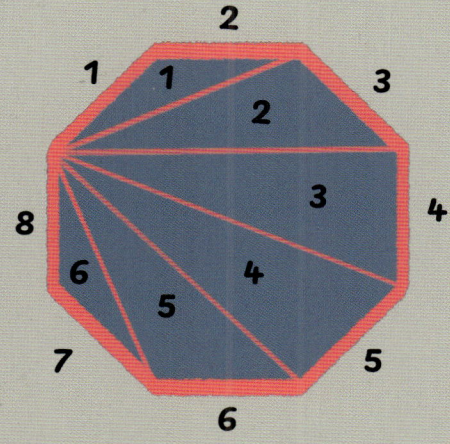

You know that all the angles in a triangle add up to 180°, so if you count up the number of triangles in a polygon and multiply by 180, you get the **total number of degrees** of the polygon's angles.

Tessellations are patterns with shapes that fit together without gaps. Triangles, squares and hexagons all make tessellations. In nature, bees' honeycombs form tessellations of interlocking hexagons.

CIRCLES AND SQUARES DON'T TESSELLATE!

IT'S OKAY – I STUCK THEM TOGETHER WITH HONEY!

Some tessellations need more than one type of regular polygon to fill the gaps. These are called **semi-regular tessellations**. They can combine triangles, squares, hexagons, octagons or dodecagons (twelve-sided polygons).

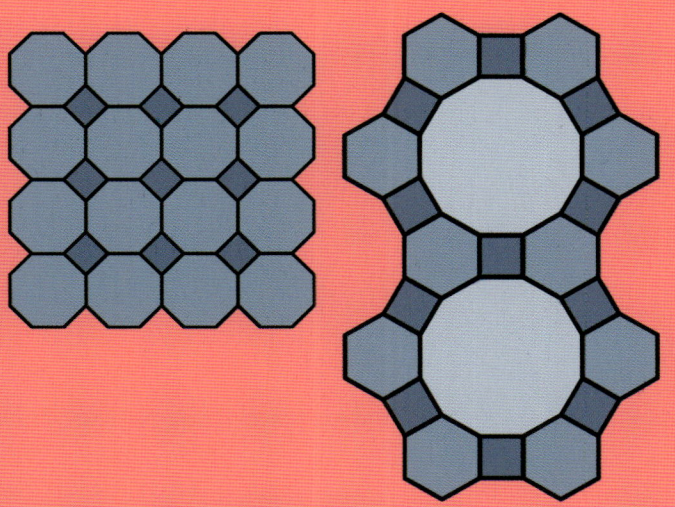

3D SHAPES

Shapes that are 3D (three-dimensional) have **length, width and depth**. They can be any size and shape, and they can be hollow or solid. Spheres, cubes, pyramids and cylinders are all 3D shapes.

WE VISITED YOUR FAMILY IN CUBA, SO NOW YOU'RE COMING TO SEE MINE IN EGYPT.

3D shapes are called **polyhedrons**, from the ancient Greek *polus* meaning **many**, and *hedra* meaning **base**.

The **Platonic solids** are five special polyhedrons that are named after the Greek philosopher Plato. Each shape has sides that are regular polygons and angles that are all the same.

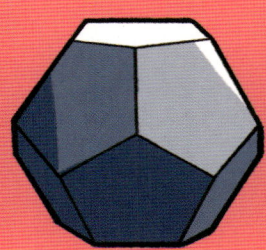

tetrahedron (four faces)

cube (six faces)

octahedron (eight faces)

dodecahedron (twelve faces)

icosahedron (twenty faces)

Bizarrely, Plato thought that the Platonic solids might be the building blocks of the universe and form the basic elements of nature – **fire, earth, air and water**.

tetrahedron = sharp = fire

cube = solid = earth

octahedron = smooth = air

icosahedron = flowing = water

The leftover dodecahedron shape was nothing less than the **arrangement of the stars in the heavens**.

HEAVENS, HUMANS ARE FULL OF HOT AIR!

In the real world, the atoms (building blocks) of diamonds really are arranged in a tetrahedron shape. This **firm structure** helps to make diamond the strongest natural material on Earth.

The Sun is considered to be the **most perfect sphere** in nature. The Earth is slightly too squashed at the Poles and bulging at the equator to be a true sphere.

A **sphere** is a round, ball-shaped solid that is perfectly symmetrical – wherever you draw a line of symmetry.

THAT'S JUST HOW I ROLL, BABY!

The **18th-century mathematician Leonhard Euler** found a formula (mathematical rule) that works for all polyhedrons with flat faces and straight edges.

Number of faces + number of corners = number of edges + 2

IS THERE AN EQUATION TO WORK OUT HOW MANY FACES I'VE GOT?

For a cube, that works out as:

6 faces + 8 corners = 14 = 12 edges + 2

Weird!

TRANSFORMATIONS

In some jobs, such as graphic design and architecture, people move shapes around without altering their basic outlines. In maths, these changes are called **transformations**.

MY UNCLE BOB COULD TRANSFORM INTO A CAR!

There are three main types of transformation – **rotation, reflection and translation**.

When you **rotate** a shape, you turn it through an angle based at a fixed point, called a centre of rotation.

Door locks, wind turbines and clock hands are all examples of objects that rotate.

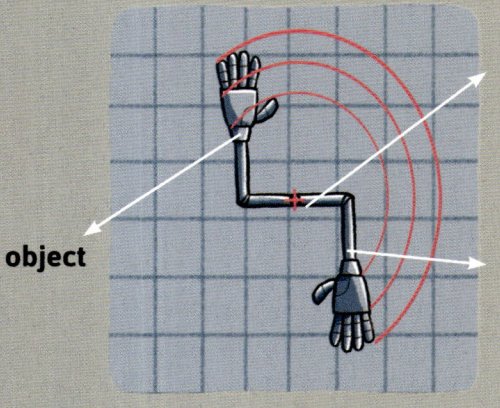

centre of rotation

object

image

The original shape is called an **object** and the new shape is an **image**.

You **reflect** a shape when you flip it over an imaginary line called a mirror line, creating an exact copy. When you look in a mirror you see a reflection.

Graphic designers sometimes **flip** images to create interesting designs.

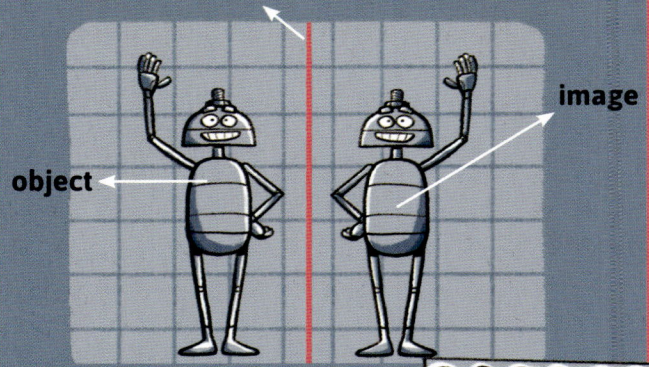

mirror line

object

image

YES, I CAN SEE MYSELF DOING THIS...

Moving a shape without rotating or reflecting it is called a **translation**. You can slide it up or down, left or right, but its appearance doesn't change in any other way.

Planes taking off and elevators moving up and down are examples of translation.

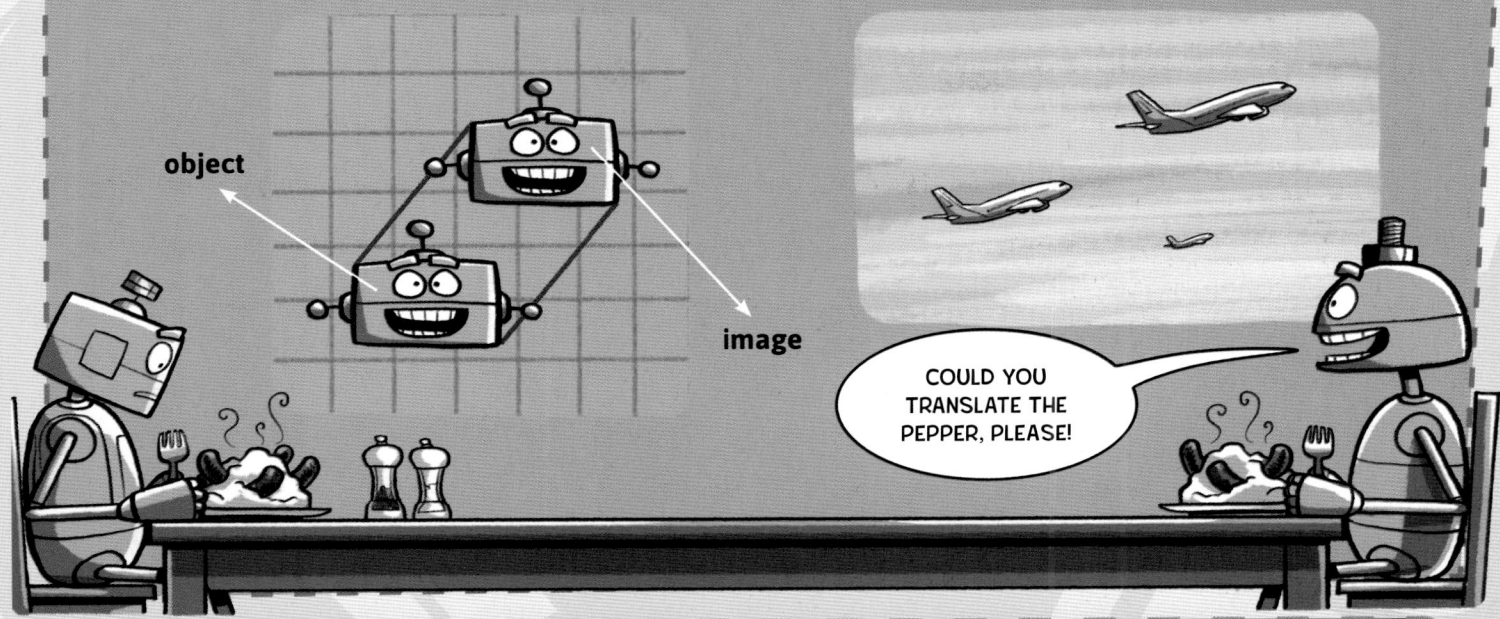

object

image

COULD YOU TRANSLATE THE PEPPER, PLEASE!

Enlargement is a type of transformation that changes the size of a shape while it otherwise stays the same. A number called a scale factor tells you how much bigger (or smaller if it is a negative number) to make the shape.

image

NOW HE'S TWICE AS CUTE!

object

scale factor = 2

ALGEBRA

Sometimes mathematicians work out calculations **even when they don't know what the numbers are**. Strange, but true! They use symbols or words instead, in a type of maths called algebra.

THOSE WEIRD MATHEMATICIANS, I BET THEY HAVE IMAGINARY FRIENDS, TOO!

The word **algebra** stems from the Arabic *al-jabr* which means **the restoring of broken parts**. It comes from a book written by the 9th-century Persian mathematician Muhammad ibn Mūsā al-Khwārizmī.

Algebra uses **equations** – statements that tell us that one quantity is equal to another. You always need to balance one side of an equation with the other. Here's an example:

$$c = 12 + 5 + 2$$

You know that **12 + 5 + 2 = 19**, so *c* must represent *19*.

Let's say there are *20* robots and six of them already have a spacecraft each to take them to the planet Algebra. To work out how many more spaceships you need to transport all the robots, you can write an equation like this:

$$6 + a = 20$$

THAT'S FINE, BUT DO WE HAVE TO GO TO PLANET ALGEBRA? COULDN'T WE GO TO PLANET ICE CREAM INSTEAD?

To find the value of *a*, first do the opposite of the equation. So instead of adding six, you subtract it. Do this on both the left and right side of the equation to balance it.

$$6 + a - 6 = 20 - 6$$

which means: $a = 20 - 6$

So, $a = 14$

When you multiply numbers in algebraic equations, you don't always use the x multiplication sign. That's because it might be confused with the algebra letter '*x*', if '*x*' is used to represent a value.

Let's say you need 80 ice lollies for the trip to Algebra and there are ten lollies in a pack. This is how you can find out how many packs are needed:

$$10 \times x = 80$$

To make it clearer, just write:

$$10x = 80$$

Then, balance the equation:

$$10x \div 10 = 80 \div 10$$

So, $x = 8$

OKAY, I'LL ACCEPT PLANET ICE LOLLY!

COORDINATES

Coordinates are sets of numbers that describe the location of a particular point. In maths, they are plotted on a coordinate grid that has two axes — 'x' and 'y' lines.

The **Cartesian system of coordinates**, which is widely used today, is named after the French philosopher René Descartes (1596–1650). The idea for coordinates came to him as he watched a fly crawling around on the ceiling and wondered how he could describe its position.

In today's world, coordinates are used in jobs such as **air-traffic control and mapmaking**.

I'M NOT SURPRISED. THAT PROBLEM WOULD REALLY BUG ME, TOO!

The **x axis** of a grid is horizontal, and the **y axis** is vertical. Let's say you want to use coordinates to describe the location of hidden treasure on the map below. First, write down how far along the location is on the x axis, then how far up it is on the y axis.

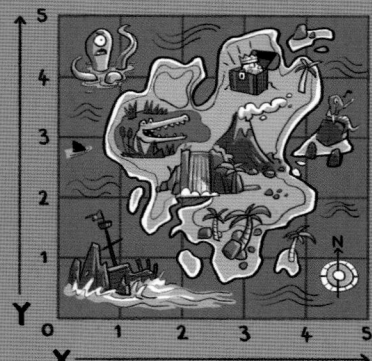

So, the coordinates for the treasure are (3, 4).

You always write the x axis number before the y axis number and separate the numbers with a comma.

To describe the location of a point below or behind '0', you extend the axes to include negative numbers. The four sections of a grid formed by the axes are called **quadrants**.

DON'T TELL THOSE LANDLUBBERS BUT I'VE ALREADY TRACKED DOWN THE BOOTY!

I KNOW THERE'S ANOTHER CRITTER AROUND HERE SOMEWHERE.

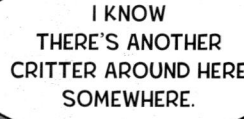

CHARTS AND GRAPHS

Mathematicians and scientists create **charts and graphs** to show and compare data clearly. Data is information collected by counting and measuring things, or by taking surveys.

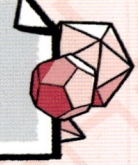

I MADE A CHART TO SHOW WHAT MOUNTAINS LOOK LIKE!

A **bar chart** is a good way to show frequency – the number of times that something occurs.

This chart displays the number of different types of pets owned by households in a street.

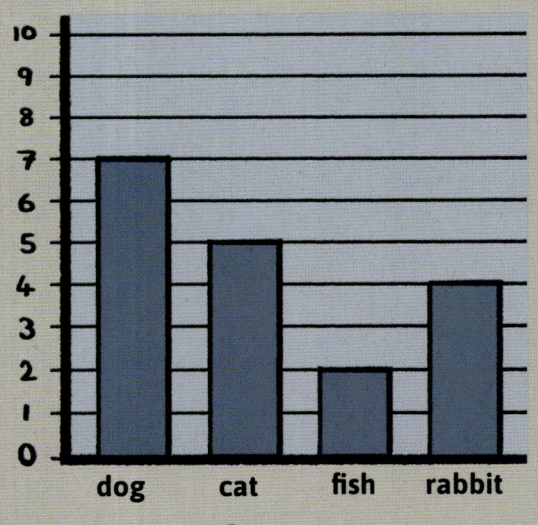

SIT, CHIP, SIT!

A **line graph** allows you to plot a trend over time.

For example, it might show the number of beach balls that have been sold over five days at a seaside stall. The data points are joined together with straight lines.

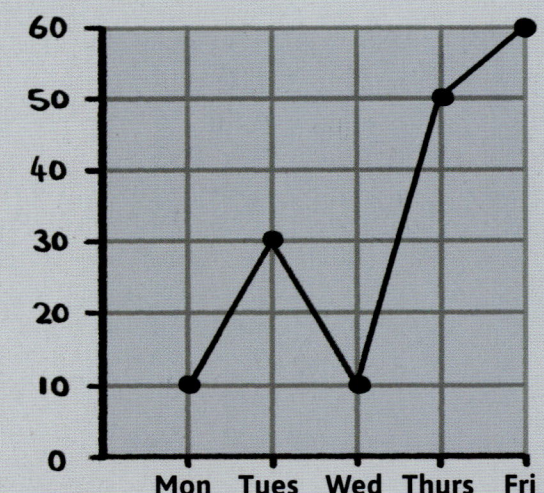

SPHERES FOR SALE! COME AND GET YOUR LOVELY PERFECTLY SYMMETRICAL, PRIMITIVE 3D SHAPES!

A **pie chart** looks like – err – a pie! Each section of it represents a category of data.

This pie chart shows the numbers of different types of robots among the *360* students at the GigaSmartZ BrainBot Academy.

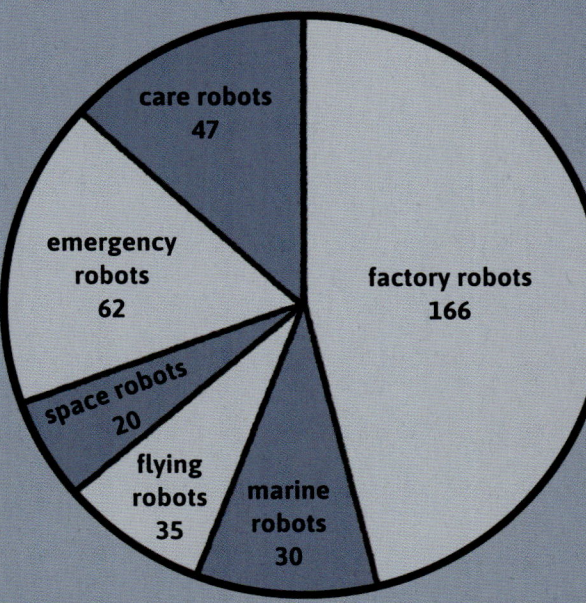

care robots
47

emergency robots
62

space robots
20

flying robots
35

marine robots
30

factory robots
166

To make a pie chart, use a compass or draw around a round object to **make a circle**. Use a protractor to mark out the sections for each robot category (placing a dot at the top of the circle as a starting point). The total number of robots is *360*, so one degree will be equal to one robot.

MORE PIE, YUMMY!

Florence Nightingale, a British nurse during the Crimean War (1853–1856), was also a talented pie chart creator. She used charts to show how unclean hospital conditions were contributing to the deaths of soldiers.

A **Venn diagram** displays the relationships between different sets of data. Let's say you have different groups, or sets, of students, such as space robots or flying robots. You write the members of these sets within curly brackets:

Space robots = {ForagerX, PiQuest, MoonBug, MArster, HoverBot}

Flying robots = {Wing800, EyeSpy, HoverBot, BuzzBird, MoonBug}

Each set is represented by a circle. If a member belongs in more than one set, it is put in the **intersection** of the two circles.

PiQuest

ForagerX

MArster

HoverBot

MoonBug

EyeSpy

Wing800

BuzzBird

space robots   **flying robots**

HoverBot and MoonBug are **both** flying robots **and** space robots.

WE'RE ALL SET. LET'S GO!

FLY ME TO THE MOON!

TOP TEN WEIRDEST MATHS FACTS

10

Long prime numbers are often used in cybersecurity to make strong online codes because they are **exceedingly difficult to crack**.

THAT'S WHAT THEY THINK!

9

The ancient Romans used letters to represent numbers. The number *1888* in Roman numerals is an extremely long **MDCCCLXXXVIII**!

8

The ancient Egyptian symbol for 100000 was a **tadpole or frog**!

HELLO AND WELCOME TO ANCIENT EGYPT'S MOST SUCCESSFUL GAME SHOW 'WHO WANTS TO BE A TEN FROGS-AIRE?'

7

A **picosecond** is a weeny amount of time – just 0.000000000001 seconds.

6

In 1299, the number *0* was **banned in Florence, Italy**, because it was thought that people could easily change it to a *9* and commit fraud.

5

It's often said that the number **7** is the world's **most popular** number. On the other hand, **13** is considered bad luck. Some hotels don't have a thirteenth floor.

I HAVE A BAD FEELING ABOUT TODAY...

4

A **googol** is an extremely large number – it's **1** followed by a hundred zeros. The search engine Google is named after it.

THAT'S MY KIND OF NUMBER!

3

The prime number **73,939,133** is very weird. You can take any number of digits off the end and you'll still have a **prime number**.

1

If you folded a thin piece of paper in half **42 times**, it would be thick enough to reach the Moon!*

WHO NEEDS ROCKETS WHEN YOU'VE GOT ORIGAMI!

* This is impossible, by the way!

2

An 80-year-old person has lived for over **2.5 billion seconds**.

THEY MUST HAVE HAD AN UPGRADE AT SOME POINT, RIGHT?

TOP MATHS ACTIVITIES

FIND THE PRIMES

Eratosthenes (c.276BC–195BC), a mathematician from (you guessed it!) ancient Greece, came up with a clever way to find prime numbers. It's called the sieve of Eratosthenes, and you can do it with colouring pens.

Trace or photocopy this grid onto a piece of paper and follow the instructions below.

1	2	3	4	5	6	7	8	9	10
11	12	13	14	15	16	17	18	19	20
21	22	23	24	25	26	27	28	29	30
31	32	33	34	35	36	37	38	39	40
41	42	43	44	45	46	47	48	49	50

1 is not a prime number, so colour it in blue.

2 is a prime number, so keep it as it is.

From 2, count every second number box and colour it in green. These are multiples of 2 so they can't be prime numbers.

3 is a prime number so skip it but then colour every third number in yellow.

Some will already be coloured in.

Leave 5 as it is, but colour in every fifth square after 5 red.

Skip 7 and colour in every seventh number after 7 in purple.

There should be fifteen numbers left that aren't coloured. These are the prime numbers under 50.

All the answers are on page 48!

46

MATCH THE NET TO THE 3D SHAPE

A net is a 2D shape that you can fold up to make a 3D solid. Can you match the correct net to each Platonic solid?

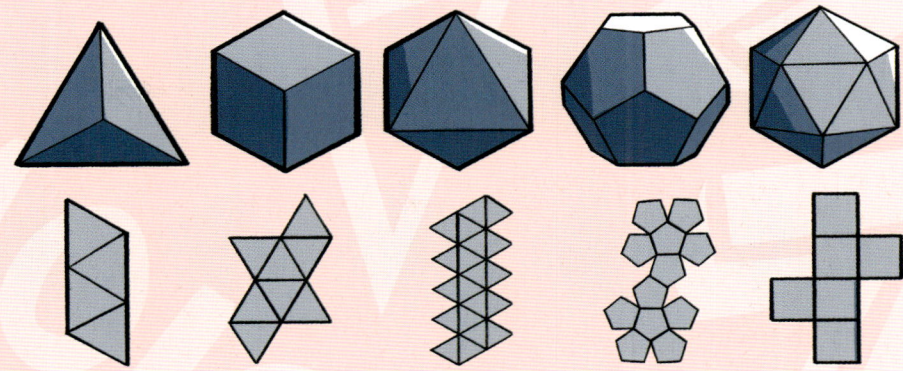

MEASURE A TREE

Here's a back-to-front but clever way to estimate the height of a tree.

1. Stand with your legs apart and your back to a tree.

2. Keeping your legs straight, bend down and look between your legs.

3. Move backwards or forwards until you just see the top of the tree.

4. The distance from your feet to the tree is about equal to the height of the tree.

5. Mark the ground where you are standing, then measure the distance along the ground to the tree, using strides, heel-to-toe steps or a tape measure.

The angle of the tree with the ground is 90° (a right angle). When you can only just see the top of the tree, the angle of sight between your legs is about 45°. This forms a right-angled isosceles triangle with two equal sides, so the distance between the tree trunk and your feet must be roughly equal to the height of the tree.

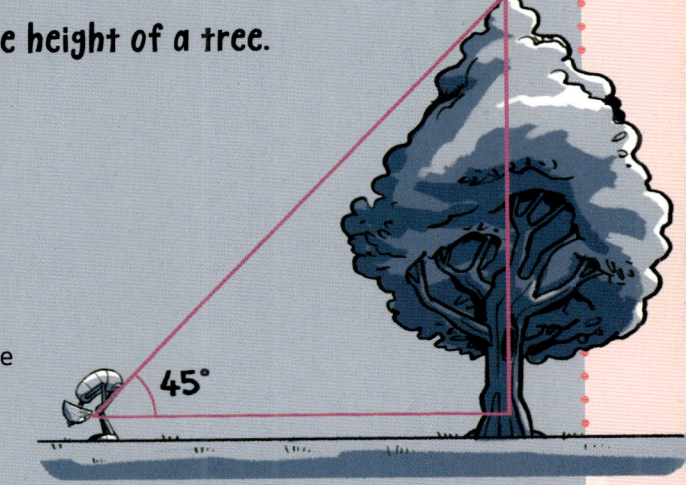

PI PLANET MISSION

The space robot PiQuest is on a mission to explore the planet Algebra and is crossing its surface, collecting rock samples. Can you work out how far it has travelled so far? Its wheels have turned 2500 times.

radius = 40 cm

INDEX

ANSWERS:

Prime Numbers:
2, 3, 5, 7, 11, 13, 17, 19, 23, 29, 31, 37, 41, 43, 47

Pi Planet Mission solution:
The radius of the robot's wheel is 40cm. So, the circumference is:
40 x 2 = 80
80 x 3.14 = 251.2cm
The distance the robot has travelled is:
2500 x 251.2cm = 628,000cm
628,000cm = 6.28km

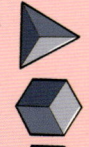

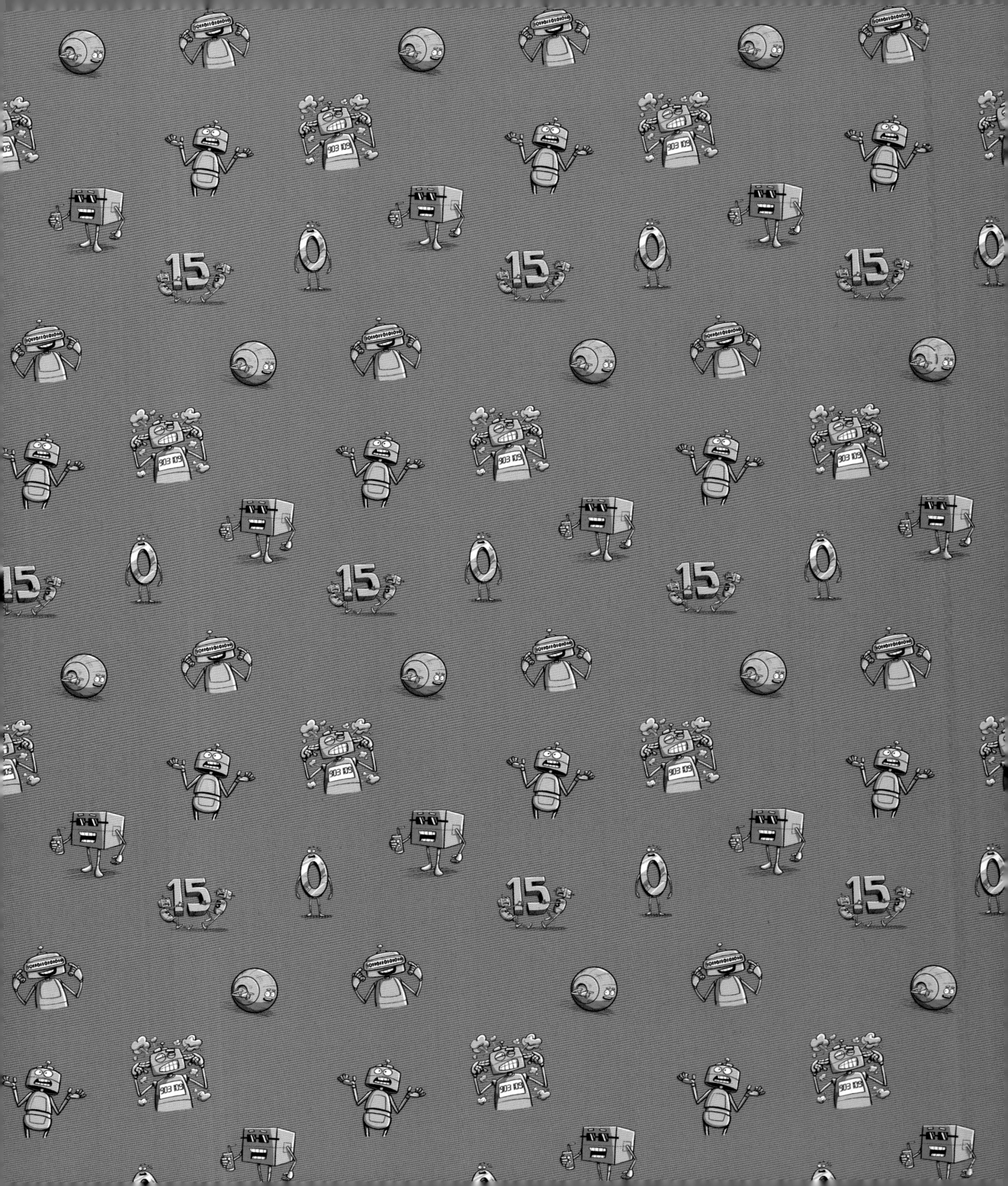

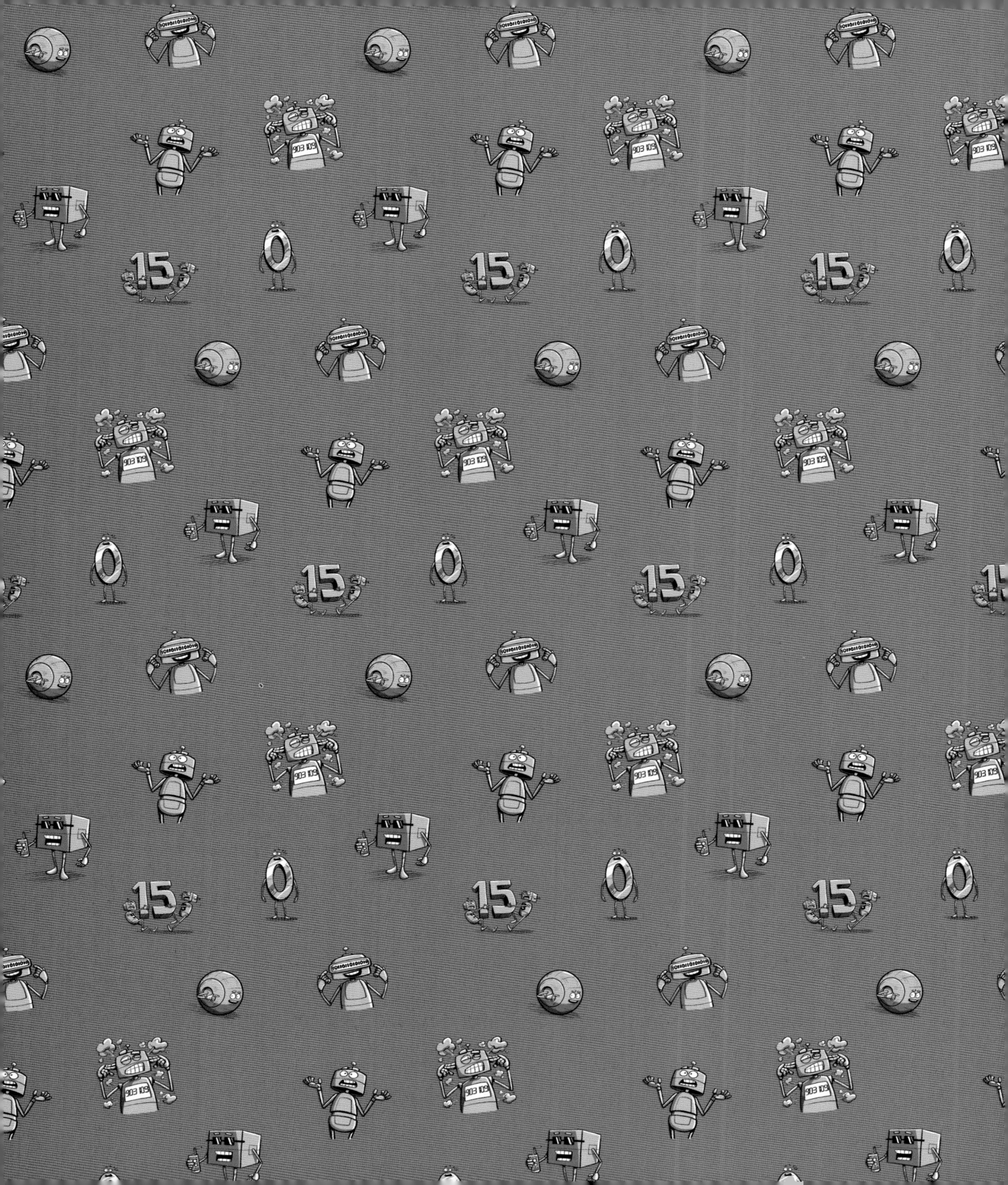